Rabbits for Beginners

ALINA DARIA

ISBN: 9798844005626

Contents

Systematics and Classification

First, it should be understood where in the animal world our domestic rabbits are scientifically classified. It is commonly known that hares and rabbits are distinguished from each other, and we will discuss the differences at a later time, yet rabbits are classified in the hare family. They, of course, belong to the class of mammals and are herein classified in the subclass of Higher Mammals (Eutheria). However, rabbits are not rodents like guinea pigs or rats, as is often wrongly assumed, but rabbits belong to the order of hares, whose scientific name is 'Lagomorpha'.

In this order two families are separated: On the one hand the hares (Leporidae) and on the other hand the whistling hares (Ochotonidae). The whistling hares are often also called pikas and represent in their family also the only genus with about thirty species, whose generic name is Ochotona. However, we do not deal with this family in this book, because our domestic rabbits belong to the other family of the order of hares: Leporidae. This name comes from Latin ('lepus' means 'hare'). So, within this family we find both hares and rabbits, however the division into hares and rabbits is not a systematic division, but there are eleven different genera belonging to this family.

The fact that there is no systematic subdivision means in this context that the respective rabbits and hares are not more closely related to each other than to the other animals from the hare family. Either several species can belong to one genus or only one species. If only one species belongs to a genus, this genus is called "monotypic" (Greek mónos = alone, typikos = typical). The genera of this family are:

Cottontail rabbits (Sylvilagus) - 13 species.

Bristled rabbit (Caprolagus hispidus) - one species

Bush rabbit (Poelagus marjorita) - one species

Bushman rabbit (Bunolagus monticularis) - one species

True hares (Lepus) - about thirty species (especially known: European hare (Lepus europaeus))

Red rabbits (Pronolagus) - 3 species

Ryukyu rabbit (Pentalagus furnessi) - one species

Striped rabbit (Nesolagus) - 2 species

Volcano rabbit (Romerolagus diazi) - one species

Wild rabbits (Oryctolagus cuniculus) - all known breeding forms of domestic rabbits are descended from this species

Dwarf rabbit (Brachylagus idahoensis) - one species

The name of an animal species always consists of the name of the associated genus, followed by the name of the respective species. Fun Fact: The genus name is always capitalized, whereas the species name that follows is always lowercase.

It is especially important to note that all known breeding forms of our domestic rabbits are descended from wild rabbits! So, they belong to the genus Oryctolagus cuniculus, although there is also a genus in the rabbit family called dwarf rabbits (Brachylagus idahoensis), but our domestic rabbits (which include our dwarf rabbits that we keep as pets) do not belong to this genus. The dwarf rabbits that live as pets are variants of domestic rabbits that were created by breeding wild rabbits. Therefore, domestic rabbits bear the scientific name "Oryctolagus cuniculus forma domestica".

Although the hare and rabbit genera within the hare family are not divided into systematic groups, there are nevertheless some characteristics that help to decide whether a particular genus should be called a "hare" or a "rabbit".

These include, for example, that rabbits usually have shorter ears than hares (relative to their respective heads) and that rabbits usually do not have as strong hind legs as hares (relative to body length). It can also be noted that rabbits tend to be smaller than hares and that hares are solitary creatures, whereas most rabbits are social creatures and live in groups.

In addition, hares are already born with fur and open eyes, whereas some rabbits are initially born blind and hairless. In direct comparison to our domestic rabbits or their wild form (the wild rabbits), it can be further noted that hares have a broader roof of the mouth as well as a shorter zygomatic process.

© Andreas Lischka Webandi

Physiology and Anatomy

Yes, rabbits are also mammals, and many bodily functions are similar to those of humans. Nevertheless, there are many differences between humans and rabbits, some of them serious, that should be known in order to better understand the animals. Let's take a closer look at this!

The dentition:

First, we need to consider what kind of animals rabbits belong to: We roughly divide animals into carnivores, herbivores, and omnivores. Rabbits belong to the herbivores, which they have in common with nearly ninety percent of all mammals. Within these groupings, rabbits can be further separated; for example, rabbits belong to the leaf-eaters, whose scientific name is "folivore."

Therefore, the rabbit's dentition is geared toward grinding plant foods (primarily leaves, but also grasses and herbs). Carnivores, on the other hand, do not need to grind their food, but have fangs and pointed molars so they can hunt down their prey and swallow it in large pieces.

Therefore, it is essential that rabbits are always well occupied with chewing their food. Anyone who has ever eaten grass knows how rich in raw fiber it is, because you have to chew the grass for what feels like endless hours before you finally swallow it. Such a long, steady and intense chewing is very important for the preservation of the molars in rabbits. Otherwise, eventually, the rabbit's teeth will grow permanently, which can lead to serious dental problems. Intensive chewing causes the upper and lower molars to grind each other down. If this does not happen and the teeth become too long, rabbits will be extremely hindered in eating and the veterinarian may have to file the teeth down.

Digestive tract:

If you already have rabbits and are not just about to get your first one, you have probably already noticed how often rabbits eat and how much they defecate accordingly. This is another reason it is so important not to anthropomorphize rabbits. Humans and rabbits are incredibly different in this regard!

Humans eat an average of two to four times a day and go to the bathroom an average of once a day. Humans can even go weeks without solid food and come out of the fasting phase perfectly healthy (or healthier!).

Rabbits, on the other hand, chow down up to eighty (!) times a day. This is not a sign of gluttony, but quite normal. They also defecate very often during the day, excreting their body's "waste" in small chunks.

Another peculiarity is that rabbits produce the so-called appendix feces. As in humans, the rabbit's food passes from the mouth into the stomach and then into the small intestine. But the rabbit has another station: the appendix. This is where vitamins and nutrients are utilized. Rabbits often eat appendix feces - this is normal and healthy. You should only be concerned if a rabbit eats a noticeable amount of feces. This may be a sign that the rabbit is not getting enough nutrients from its diet and needs to "get" them elsewhere. Or the rabbit may have an increased need due to a disease.

So, the appendix is extremely important to a rabbit - quite unlike humans, who do not depend on their appendix! A rabbit's appendix can be a full forty centimeters in length. The large intestine is also important, of course; this is about one meter long. This is where the typical small, hard rabbit droppings are produced, which, unlike the nutritious appendix droppings, are not eaten.

Eyes:

The eyes of a rabbit are located on the side of the upper part of the head. Since the two eyes are each on one side, the rabbit's field of vision is also very different from that of humans. By means of both eyes, the rabbit can see in all directions, which is extremely important for a flight animal (i.e., an animal that must keep away from predators). This enables the rabbit to recognize approaching enemies at an early stage and to quickly look for an escape route.

The field of vision of almost 360° is therefore essential for rabbits to survive in the wild. The "quality" of their vision, on the other hand, is not particularly good, because they are rather short-sighted. However, this is not a bad thing for rabbits, because they do not need eagle eyes, but only need to be able to perceive movements of predators and the like to nimbly get to safety.

For this reason, one should approach a rabbit on if possible not from behind and not from above, because this reminds rabbits of attacks by predators - even if our domestic rabbits have never experienced this in the wild, it is nevertheless embedded in their instincts. At best, the human hand approaches from the front and/or side at the same level.

Nose:

The olfactory organ of rabbits is also very different from our olfactory organ, which is nowhere near as well developed as that of our little friends! One example is that we humans have just under six million receptor cells in our nose - which sounds quite a lot, but rabbits have about fifty million! This is - like the field of vision, which covers almost 360° - extremely important for rabbits, because they can, for example, scent predators before they get to see them.

But rabbits do not only use their smelling organ for this purpose, because they also explore their environment strongly by sniffing. This also applies to their rabbit friends, whom they sniff, which they can recognize by smell and much more. Even as babies, rabbits take advantage of their great sense of smell by using this to find their mother's teats to drink milk.

A typical characteristic of the rabbit nose is the constant "twitching" of the nose. What looks simply cute to us is extremely important for the rabbit to survive, because this not only sucks air into the nose to fill up on fresh oxygen, but also allows them to recognize enemies and friends - as already described above. The twitching of the rabbit's nose is similar to the widening of our nostrils when we smell intensely or breathe more intensely, but it is usually more noticeable - and cuter!

Ears:

Also, the sense of hearing is - just like the sense of smell - much better developed than in us humans! Rabbits hear much better than we do, because they cannot only hear all the sounds that we can hear, but also sounds at higher frequencies and many bird calls, bug noises, electrical noises, mechanical noises, and so on. While humans can perceive sound waves with a frequency of up to about 20,000 hertz, rabbits are able to perceive sound waves with a frequency of at least 33,000 hertz; some rabbits even up to 49,000 hertz.

Therefore, hearing is at least as important to rabbits as smelling - if anything, it's even more important! Hearing also provides a rabbit with early warning of enemies, explores its environment, and makes great use of it for orientation. So, while we humans rely primarily on our eyes, rabbits tend to focus more on their sense of smell and hearing. Even at rest, rabbits are always alert through their ears, even when they let them rest in a relaxed manner and do not raise them. But why are a rabbit's ears exceptionally long?

Well, the most likely reason is that this allows the rabbit to hide from enemies in the grass or bushes, but at the same time still hear perfectly through the erect ears. Therefore, many rabbits with floppy ears do not do quite as well in the wild as their counterparts with erect ears, which, moreover, they can move in different directions - even independently of each other. In addition, rabbits also perceive sounds far away; how far away the sound can be to still be perceived by a rabbit depends on the particular sound, of course, but if the sound is perceptible enough, it can sometimes be heard by a rabbit even 3 kilometers away.

Breathing:

It is very important to know that rabbits breathe through their nose. Yes, we humans breathe through the nose, but we also use the mouth for breathing. This is not the case with rabbits, as mouth breathing is virtually ineffective in rabbits - this is one of the reasons why colds are so dangerous for rabbits (apart from the fact that rabbits are more sensitive than humans and that a cold can quickly develop into pneumonia). For example, if the nose is blocked by a disease, this is extremely dangerous for rabbits. Here, preventive and early action must be taken, because when the rabbit begins to suck in air through the mouth, it already suffers from severe respiratory distress!

© *Christel Chiem Seherin*

Getting the Rabbits

When looking to acquire a pet, many people's first path leads them to a pet store. This idea is firmly entrenched in the minds of many people, even though there are better and more pet-friendly options than the traditional pet store. The more people are educated about the practices of many pet stores, the more they distance themselves from them and are more likely to seek out animal shelters, foster homes and even reputable breeders.

Pet stores are commercial enterprises that want to make a profit just like any other business. Therefore, animals are considered commodities in many pet stores and are treated as such. Granted, this is not true of all pet stores, and there are also many employees who continue their education and treat the animals well! Nevertheless, making a profit comes first.

In very many cases, the animals offered in pet shops come from dubious mass breeding farms, where the animals are "produced" under undignified conditions. The word "production" unfortunately fits very well here, as the animals are often regarded as products and not as living beings with special needs.

This is now quite well documented and there is an abundance of footage from such breeding operations. Here, as a rule, very little emphasis is placed on species-appropriate husbandry and breeding. This is not only the case with rabbits, but also with many other animal species that are offered in the pet trade, such as hamsters, guinea pigs, rats, etc.

In many cases, the animals have far too little space, are fed unhealthy and cheap food, and often develop diseases. Dead animals are sometimes not removed, and the enclosures are often cleaned too rarely. Many animals in pet shops therefore show diseases, either due to genetic defects, as serious breeding requires a lot of expertise, or due to the poor keeping conditions in the breeding farms.

Often the young animals are separated from their mothers much too early in order to sell them early and make a profit. Therefore, it is always important to know the origin of the respective rabbits.

A young animal should be allowed to stay with its mother for at least twelve weeks, sixteen weeks would be even better - on the one hand because the baby rabbits still need their mother's milk and on the other hand because they develop and are taught their social behavior during this time. In addition, the kittens also eat their mother's appendix feces, and this is important for the development of a healthy immune system as well as intestinal flora.

Regarding the males, it is important to mention that they are already sexually mature from the age of twelve weeks and could theoretically already mate their sisters or even their own mother. This must of course be avoided. If the males are to remain in the group, however, early castration can prevent the little males from having to be separated from their female comrades, because early castration, in contrast to "normal" castration, takes place before the young animal's testicles descend.

Now it is only logical and understandable to feel sorry for the animals in the pet shop. Considering the circumstances, many people do not realize that these animals often suffer, or they want to save them. The thought is commendable. However, one must remember that these practices are supported with every purchase, even if the purchase was made out of compassion and love for the animals.

In capitalism, demand strongly determines supply. If we now imagine that no one would buy animals from dubious mass breeding companies or from classic pet shops anymore, this business model would no longer be profitable, and breeders and pet shops would be forced to change their handling of animals. Either the mass animal trade would slowly die out or the companies would have to massively improve their practices to generate demand again. So, it is in the power of every single animal lover to improve the fate of animals born in the future.

Now the question is where to source rabbits and other pets with a clear conscience. The best options are animal shelters on the one hand and foster/rescue homes on the other. Both shelters and foster homes have many animals that were unwanted or abandoned by their previous owners. Therefore, the most logical and sensible thing to do is to first offer these animals a new, nice home. Serious breeders are also a possibility, but many people think it makes more sense to first give the already existing animals (in animal shelters and foster homes) a new chance, instead of breeding more and more animals, of which then a certain part ends up in emergency stations and animal shelters again.

In animal shelters and foster homes, you often find somewhat older or adult animals. But also, here there are young animals, which for example come from unwanted mating and were then abandoned. Or they were arbitrarily given away for Christmas, but ultimately not wanted. Some of these animals are quite easy to care for, others are a bit more difficult; which is often also due to the fact that many animals in shelters and emergency stations have experienced no or little love in the past.

Especially for beginners, foster homes are in many cases preferable to animal shelters, because foster homes can often offer better advice and also aftercare than animal shelters. Shelters mainly take care of dogs and cats, so knowledge about rabbits is sometimes quite limited - although of course this does not apply to all shelters! Foster homes, on the other hand, are run by people who often have years of experience caring for the species in question. Many foster homes focus on a specific species, or at least a few different species. Therefore, the operators of such foster homes are usually very good contacts who are happy to provide advice and assistance, which is especially advantageous for newcomers.

Serious breeders are also a suitable alternative, but they are to be strictly distinguished from pure breeders. Serious breeders know their animals very well, they know the pedigrees, have profound knowledge in biology and genetics. This does not apply to pure breeders, because they often put the animals together without a well thought out plan and then sell the kittens without taking care of the future home.

In addition, it should not be forgotten that in addition to the purchase of the rabbits and the acquisition of the initial equipment, there are also running costs, for example, for hay, bedding, food. Also, care should be taken to always have enough money in case a rabbit gets sick and needs to go to the vet. Veterinary costs can be quite high and also add up quickly if the rabbit needs surgery, for example.

© *Esi Grünhagen Fee Loona*

Genders and Groups

The most important thing already in advance: Beginners should please not breed animals and also not take the risk that the animals can reproduce unintentionally. Breeding should be reserved for very experienced people who can draw on years of experience and have extensive knowledge regarding genetics.

There are now several group constellations, some of which are more and others less suitable for newcomers.

A male rabbit must of course be neutered before living with a female to prevent the pair from reproducing.

In principle, a rabbit should never be kept alone, as rabbits are extremely social animals. They need at least one companion of the same species to live a happy life. If a rabbit is kept alone, behavioral problems and often unfortunately depression, immune deficiency due to loneliness, often premature death, etc. will occur.

Some people like to keep a rabbit alone, because the animal then clings to the human as the only "reference person", but this is in no way species appropriate. How would we feel if we had only rabbits as friends and were never allowed to seek contact with another human?

© *Angela Vampy 24*

Even older rabbits are in most cases still easily socializable and can be socialized with other rabbits, since rabbits are generally quite peaceful animals, especially when they live in a pair with an opposite-sex partner (i.e., when a neutered male lives with a female). When socializing rabbits, in most cases there are much fewer problems than with some other species, for example, socializing chinchillas, which is often already more difficult.

Rabbits must be kept at least in pairs; the most popular and uncomplicated constellation is to keep a neuter with a female, because experience shows that there are fewer conflicts between males and females than between two males or two females. Yes, of course there are also many cases where two males or two females get along great with each other, but in same-sex constellations there are more disputes overall than in opposite-sex pairs. Particularly during puberty, there are more frequent and sometimes extreme disputes in same-sex couples. Puberty in rabbits lasts from about the sixth to the tenth month of life.

Even a group of three can be recommended to a beginner with a clear conscience. If you want to keep a group of four or more rabbits, it is advisable to gain experience in rabbit keeping first, because disputes are more likely to occur in a larger group. If you already have a lot of experience with rabbits and decide to keep a larger group, it is recommended to keep an even number of group members (e.g., two neutered males with two females or three neutered males with three females), because experience shows that this is more harmonious than an odd number of rabbits.

Nevertheless, these are only guidelines based on general experience and are by no means applicable to every group, because every rabbit has its own individual character and personality. Not every rabbit has a good relationship with every other rabbit - it is safest if the rabbits already know each other from an early age, although even here (especially during puberty) sometimes violent disputes can occur. It is a bit comparable with us humans: We also do not have a good relationship with every other person. It is the same with rabbits, some rabbits love each other idolatrously, some get along well, and some just can't stand each other - for reasons that are sometimes not even apparent to us. In addition, there are rabbits that are quite comfortable in a large group, and rabbits that prefer to live with just one other friend. Some rabbits are very active and full of energy, while other rabbits need a lot of rest and can be annoyed by too active companions.

Which group size and group composition are therefore suitable for the respective owner is an individual decision and always also depends on how much space the future owner can provide for the rabbits and which possibly already existing pairs or groups are available?

Furthermore, it is important to mention that not every castration is the same: there is on the one hand the "early castration" and on the other hand the "normal castration". Early castration is performed before the male becomes fertile, among other things so that he can stay longer with his mom or in his existing group. Since the male is not yet fertile at this time, the animal is immediately allowed to return to its mother and the rest of the group. In addition, early neutering is considered easier than normal neutering and experience has shown that there are fewer complications.

Normal neutering can be done at any time, but of course should not be done on particularly old or sick animals if possible. Neutering tends to be a rather simple and routine operation, however, like any operation, it involves stress and a residual risk. After a normal castration, the male remains capable of procreation for some time, as there are still sperm in the seminal vesicle, which are only gradually degraded.

In addition, we should briefly mention the combination of a rabbit and a guinea pig, as this composition has been very popular for many years. The combination of a rabbit and a guinea pig goes well in many cases (apparently!), since both animals usually do not act exceptionally aggressive, but it is anything but species appropriate. Not all animals are the same - because rabbits and guinea pigs do not speak the same language and cannot communicate (properly) with each other. This composition is no better than keeping them individually.

Both animal species are social creatures that need at least one friend of the same species (!) to live a happy life. This composition doesn't make sense anyway, because if you get two animals, you can choose either two rabbits or two guinea pigs (instead of a combination of the two). However, you often see rabbits and guinea pigs living peacefully together in a large group - this is not a problem in most cases, as long as there is no aggression between the animals and as long as each species also has companions of the same species!

However, whether the rabbits living together in a group have the same breed, the same size, or the same ears (floppy ears vs. standing ears) does not play a role in whether the rabbits get along. Much more important, as explained above, is whether the characters match. Age is also of secondary importance, although it should be mentioned that preferably rabbits should live together that have approximately the same age.

For example, if you put a very old rabbit together with a young animal, where the young animal is still very (hyper-)active and the old animal already needs a lot of rest, this can lead to problems, because the old animal can quickly be annoyed by the young animal's verve and the young animal might get bored if the old animal does not want to play (anymore).

© K Nyaka

The Rabbit Home

Rabbits need a lot of space and at least one friend of the same species! Gone are the days when rabbits were kept lonely and alone in a small cage. Fortunately! In the meantime, the knowledge about the species-appropriate attitude of rabbits is spreading more and more, but unfortunately many myths still persist around the rabbit attitude and outdated attitude forms are mediated above all by large pet supply enterprises further to so far ignorant new owners.

Since most people keep their rabbits indoors or outdoors, we will place our focus on indoor husbandry and only touch on outdoor husbandry in passing.

First, it must be remembered that rabbits want and need to move around a lot! No one wants to be confined to a small area, not even rabbits, which by nature have a great urge to move, scampering around a lot and often, jumping around, hooking, etc. Therefore, the rabbits should be provided with a sufficiently large enclosure including regular exercise, although very many owners also practice free housing, where the rabbits are allowed to move freely in the entire (or almost the entire) apartment and have a place of retreat and their toilet in a certain place. Whether this is an option for the respective owner is always an individual decision and there must also be a risk assessment, because there must of course be no hazards in the form of other pets (dogs, cats), stairs or other fall opportunities, etc. Also, the entire home must be made rabbit proof. Therefore, most people choose to keep them in an enclosure with regular exercise under supervision.

If the living conditions allow it, the rabbits can of course also be provided with a whole rabbit room in which they can move freely. However, we start here from the most common form of husbandry: From the attitude in an enclosure.

Recommendations for the minimum space rabbits should have vary from country to country. For example, in Germany, the guidelines of the TVT, whose abbreviation stands for the Veterinary Association for Animal Welfare, are used as a guide. This is not a law in its own right, but since the Animal Welfare Act stipulates that pets must be housed in a manner appropriate to their species and that their need for exercise must be met, the recommendations of the Veterinary Association for Animal Welfare are often consulted in court.

Sufficient space is essential for both mental and physical health. In enclosures that are too small, fights can occur more often because the animals can't get out of each other's way, the animals are more prone to obesity because they can't get enough exercise, they sometimes develop depression due to the lack of space, and more.

The recommendations for rabbits are written down in the leaflet No. 131.5 of the Veterinary Association for Animal Welfare. On page 4 of leaflet No. 131.5, it is stated that rabbits should have at least six to eight square meters at their free disposal. This applies to two rabbits. For each additional rabbit, two to three square meters should be added. So according to TVT, for example, a group of four rabbits should be given at least ten square meters of space. That sounds a lot, and it is a lot - ten square meters can be a small rabbit room. Nevertheless, it is important not to ignore these minimum recommendations, as too little space and exercise can lead to serious illness and also depression.

For many people, therefore, the free housing is easier - and also nicer, because so you can live "properly" with the animals together. A retreat with hiding places, toilet and feeding place the rabbits need of course nevertheless.

The enclosure may also be built over two floors, so that the rabbits have even more space available. The prerequisite for this is, of course, that the animals do not fall anywhere and could injure themselves.

With self-built enclosures should also be ensured that the floor is protected and that no urine, etc. can penetrate to the outside. If the enclosure is made of wood, special care should of course be taken that the wood does not rot and mold due to wetness or the like. For insulation, therefore, pond liner is particularly popular, as it is very waterproof and at the same time not too expensive.

Furthermore, it can be cut well and easily, depending on how much pond liner you need and in what shape.

Since rabbits have a high need to dig, they should also be offered a box for digging with lots of sand as well as plenty of straw and hay, so that rabbits can follow their urge to build nests or burrows. At best, the sand in the burrowing box should be layered at least half a meter high. The burrowing box can be set up very easily - all you need is a high box, for example made of hard plastic, which the rabbits should not gnaw on, otherwise wooden boxes or similar material are of course also suitable. Some keepers also fill the crate with soil, but for hygienic reasons I would prefer sand - conventional, fine play sand or even bird sand is best. To add a bit of variety, the crate can be spiced up with hay, straw, paper, kitchen paper, scraps of fabric and the like!

© *Marzena P.*

For the substrate, normal small animal bedding is usually used in the rabbit enclosure, which can be found in any pet store. Normal small animal bedding (wood shavings from soft wood, e.g., pine or spruce) is very absorbent and provides the animals with a fairly soft surface. However, coconut litter, for example, is often used as it is also very absorbent, but it is important to check if the rabbits eat it. Eaten coconut litter can lead to severe blockages. Hemp litter is also quite popular as this is completely dust free, but usually has poorer absorbency than conventional small animal litter. If you want to use wood pellets, which are actually very good at absorbing urine and binding odors, be sure to use another soft bedding over the wood pellets, as the wood pellets are not at all comfortable for rabbits' feet! In addition, the bedding must not contain any fragrances, but must remain very natural.

Furthermore, rabbits need enough hiding places. While many rabbits will cuddle with each other if they get along particularly well, this is not always the case. However, even though some rabbits like to cuddle with each other, each rabbit should have at least one hiding place so that the animals can get out of each other's way when they need their rest.

Therefore, each rabbit should have at least one hutch so they can get out of each other's way and rest when they want to. Rabbits have a hierarchy. Therefore, they will not strictly divide the houses among themselves, but often change the place, however, it may happen that a higher-ranking rabbit drives another animal out of a certain house because it wants to relax there itself - then the lower-ranking animal must make room.

Also, other retreat possibilities can be offered gladly, for example hammocks are usually very popular! There are hardly any limits to the imagination here, provided the materials are non-toxic and safe for the animals.

For occupation, the rabbits can also be offered many different things - you can also get a little creative. For example, rabbits love to run through tunnels and explore new objects. Some examples:

- Willow bridges
- Branches of non-toxic trees (e.g., apple trees, birch, beech or hazelnut bushes)
- Tunnels and tubes made of cardboard, cork, untreated wood, etc.
- Intelligence toys
- Food toys (e.g., food balls)

Opinions differ on the question of whether food bowls are necessary. Few rabbits leave their food in the bowl and pull it out anyway before eating it. I do not use feeding bowls and instead distribute the food in the cage. However, rabbits should always have access to fresh drinking water, although most rabbits don't drink much (or anything) anyway if they are fed a species-appropriate diet. In the wild, rabbits get their fluid needs almost exclusively from the food they eat, i.e., grass, leaves, herbs, etc. If rabbits are fed pellets or other dry food, this obviously does not correspond to the diet in the wild and the animals have to drink (a lot of) additional water to avoid dehydration. However, even with a species-appropriate, natural diet, fresh drinking water should always be available for the rabbits to help themselves to if they wish.

In this regard, there is an age-old debate: which is better, drinking bottles or drinking bowls?

I personally offer only bowls and recommend this. At first glance, a drinking bottle may seem more hygienic, since the water in the bottle does not come into contact with litter, food or the like. However, in my experience, bowls are more hygienic than bottles because they are much easier to clean. A bowl can be easily rinsed, you can get to all the corners and cleaning with vinegar water (antibacterial!) is also easy.

All bowls should be made of ceramic or a similar material to prevent chewing. Plastic bowls should be avoided. In addition, ceramic bowls are more stable and do not tip over as easily.

Drinking bottles, on the other hand, can grow all sorts of germs - and even algae. Cleaning is more difficult, and you need a special brush to reach the corners. Furthermore, cleaning the nipple is a hurdle because this is often where most deposits form. Especially the small ball in the nipple drinkers is hard to reach or to clean satisfactorily.

Some rabbit owners offer both options and first observe whether the animals prefer a bottle or a bowl. In any case, the drinking place must be cleaned daily, and fresh water must be offered every day.

Whether tap water can be used for this purpose usually varies from country to country and even from region to region, because the quality of tap water depends on many factors. If the tap water is of good drinking quality and does not contain chlorine, it can be used for the rabbits; otherwise, it is better to use bottled water.

Salt licks, on the other hand, are completely unnecessary and often do more harm than good, as the excess salt can put extreme stress on the kidneys. If necessary, there is an "oversupply" of sodium chloride, which in the worst case can even lead to kidney failure.

No animal needs a salt lick, because in a species-appropriate diet the animals get the required salts and other minerals and vitamins anyway. It is often overestimated how much salt an animal (or a human) needs, because the required amounts are quite small and can easily be covered by a species-appropriate diet. Delicious herbs are particularly well suited for this purpose!

Also, it is not possible to control which rabbit uses the salt lick how often and how intensively - if you only lick it from time to time, this is not a major problem, but some animals nibble at the stones and bite off much too large chunks. In combination with the fact that the required nutrients are covered by a healthy diet anyway, it is better to leave salt lick stones alone.

However, rabbits do need 24/7 access to hay, of which there should only be exceptions if the rabbits have 24/7 access to fresh grass - because hay is dried grass, and this is the basis of their entire diet! But we will look at this in more detail in a separate chapter.

In addition, it is important that the rabbit enclosure is in a protected and safe place: there should be no drafts and direct sunlight should also be avoided.

Rabbits can become quite housebroken with a bit of training, which makes keeping them a bit less of a hassle than keeping guinea pigs, for example, who spread their droppings all over the place - not because they are unhygienic animals, but because guinea pigs have a hard time controlling whether a droppings falls out. Therefore, they often urinate and defecate where they feel most comfortable (at the sleeping place or while feeding), and even lose a pellet while walking. Rabbits are more housebroken in this regard, as they too can have a mishap from time to time, but they get used to their litter box quite well, especially if it is lined with soft, comfortable bedding and if they are shown where the droppings and pee belong. To do this, you can collect the droppings from the enclosure and wet bedding and put them in the toilet, so that the rabbits learn where the "garbage" belongs. It is also possible to offer two toilets, so that several rabbits can "go to the toilet" at the same time.

© Robert Balog Bergadder

Diet and Nutrition

We have already briefly touched on it before animals are divided into carnivores, herbivores, to which almost 90% of mammals belong, and omnivores. In this there are often further specializations, for example insectivores belong to carnivores and leaf-eaters belong to herbivores.

Rabbits are pure herbivores whose natural diet is largely based on leaves. In addition to leaves, they also eat grasses, wild herbs and the like. Our goal is to replicate the natural diet as closely as possible in our pets as well. Fun Fact: The diets of popular pets rabbits and guinea pigs are very similar and both species eat both leaves and grasses, but in the wild rabbits feed mostly on leaves while guinea pigs feed mostly on grasses. However, both are essential for both animals.

In advance I would like to point out that I have already published a special nutrition book ("Bunny Tummy – species appropriate nutrition for rabbits"). On about 110 pages we discuss species-appropriate food and take a closer look at plant food. The topic of nutrition is very complex, but also the be-all and end-all of giving rabbits a long and healthy life. We will look at nutrition in this chapter, but for more detailed information, I refer you to the guidebook mentioned above.

As previously mentioned, rabbits in the wild eat mainly leaves, grass and wild herbs. This is why it is so important that hay is available to rabbits around the clock - because hay is nothing more than dried grass (often enriched with dried herbs or flowers).

If you live in a region where it is still quite warm in the winter, you can offer animals fresh grass, fresh leaves and fresh wild herbs all year round, but for most of us this is not the case - so hay is a "substitute" for the rabbit's staple food.

It is extremely important for rabbits to eat food often, which has a high percentage of raw fiber and must be chewed very well. The rabbit's teeth continue to grow steadily - unlike those of us humans - and must be well abraded by chewing.

In the past, it was often thought that tooth wear happened by feeding hard food, so many rabbits were given hard bread and the like at the time. However, this is anything but healthy, as this food already softens quickly in the mouth, does not need to be chewed well, and is often heavy in the stomach.

It is better if rabbits eat a lot of raw fiber-rich and low-calorie food. This is because tooth wear takes place through intense chewing, where the teeth rub against each other. If rabbits don't have enough to chew, they are at risk of dental problems!

However, it should always be noted that rabbit digestion is much more sensitive than our human digestion - this means that any new food must be fed slowly at first so that the body gets used to the new food.

If it is warm enough and you offer your rabbits fresh grass, it is possible that they will hardly notice their hay during this time - because hay is just dried grass.

Therefore, many rabbits prefer to choose the fresh variety. Nevertheless, hay should always be offered and freely available around the clock.

Furthermore, you should keep in mind that rabbits usually pick out the best stalks in the hay. It is normal for rabbits not to eat all the hay provided. They should be allowed to pick the most valuable stalks and leave the rest. Therefore, you should provide new hay daily, even if the old hay from the previous day has not been (completely) eaten.

Under no circumstances should you "force" the animals to eat everything before there is a refill.

Hay should always be stored in a dry place. It should not come into contact with moisture. It should also be stored in a dark place - for example, a wooden box, cardboard boxes or cloth bags are optimal for storage, as the hay can still "breathe".

If you want to search for fresh food for your rabbits in a nearby forest, along field paths or similar places, you should make sure that no rat poisons or similar have been sprayed here. This is also important if, for example, you are sourcing food from a family member's or friend's garden. Also, no food should be collected from busy roads or the like, because of course the exhaust pollution is high here.

Rabbits also enjoy tasty wild herbs that provide all sorts of different vitamins and minerals. You can learn more about the individual herbs in my special nutrition guide. The following wild herbs are great for feeding your animals:

- Dandelion
- Nettles
- Daisies
- Clover
- Ribwort and plantain
- Chamomile
- bedstraw
- Groundsel
- dock
- Watercress
- Goutweed
- St. John's wort

- Yarrow
- Cranesbill
- Chickweed
- Bird Vetch

This list is of course not exhaustive but contains only examples.

Kitchen herbs can also be happily fed, for example:

- Basil

- Parsley (not to pregnant females)

- dill

- coriander

- marjoram

- oregano

- Mint

- Sage

- Thyme

However, there are plants that should not be fed under any circumstances. Some plants are even deadly, both to rabbits and to humans - these include meadow saffron and lily of the valley. Other poisonous plants include ferns, lilies, oleander, belladonna, etc. Therefore, if you find a new plant that is not mentioned in the lists, you must always research whether it is edible at all.

Many rabbits also readily accept tree leaves. For example, the leaves of beech, birch and hazel are often particularly popular. Also suitable are the leaves of apple trees, apricot trees, pear trees, cherry trees, peach trees and many others. It is a common myth that the leaves of fruit trees should not be fed because they contain prussic acid. This myth has been disproved many times (e.g., by Dr. Kupper of the University of Zurich), but unfortunately it still circulates. Amygdalin is only contained in the seeds/stones of the respective fruits, for example in the seeds of the cherry and the plum. No amygdalin is found in the fruits themselves, nor in the twigs or leaves. They can therefore be offered without any problems. (Amygdalin is a cyanogenic glycoside that breaks down prussic acid in the presence of water and the enzyme mixture emulsin).

But even here there are some tree species that are toxic to rabbits - for example, boxwood, yew, elder, magnolia, and others.

Also, very suitable for feeding your rabbits are leafy vegetables, especially many different types of lettuce! Especially healthy are bitter lettuces, as they offer the most nutrients.

Lettuce varieties such as iceberg lettuce or lettuce are also not harmful and can be eaten quietly, but they offer little added value and contain a lot of nitrates. The money paid for vegetables can therefore be better invested in the following lettuces:

- Endive
- Radicchio
- Frisée
- Chicory

- Romaine lettuce

- Lollo rosso

- Lamb's lettuce

Supermarkets and weekly markets can also often provide free or inexpensive green fodder, which is perfect for consumption, but is not usually used by humans. These include:

- Kohlrabi leaves
- Carrot greens
- Cauliflower leaves
- Radish leaves
- Celery leaves

Now we come to a somewhat controversial topic: cabbage! Many people demonize cabbage because it is (supposedly) flatulent. However, this is only true if some other points in the diet are not correct. If rabbits are fed a species-appropriate diet of fresh food and hay, feeding cabbage is not a problem either and is very suitable for cold winters.

However, cabbage can cause regurgitation if pellets or industrial dry food are fed at the same time. This food is not part of the rabbits' natural diet, as their diet is based on fresh food that is chewed well and thoroughly. This is not the case with pellets and industrial dry food, especially if there are also unhealthy additives such as molasses, vegetable by-products, grains, etc. in this food. None of this is healthy or species appropriate for rabbits.

If cabbage is fed, it must be started slowly, just like any other new food. If changes in feeding are made too quickly, digestive problems can always occur because the rabbit's digestion has not had enough time to adapt to the new food.

Therefore, the same applies to cabbage: Please feed slowly over several days. For example, the first day you can offer a fingernail-sized piece, the next day a finger-sized piece, the next day a leaf, and so on. Assuming, of course, your rabbits respond well to the new food.

There are some cabbage varieties that are quite high in high molecular weight carbohydrates and therefore should be fed infrequently. These cabbages can actually promote regurgitation if eaten in excessive amounts and/or if a particular rabbit has a sensitive digestion. These cabbages are also high in water-binding fiber, another reason they should be eaten in moderation. They are Brussels sprouts, red cabbage, white cabbage and savoy cabbage.

The following cabbages are wonderful for feeding to rabbits:

- Kale (the absolute leader among cabbages and insanely healthy for rabbits and humans).

- Kohlrabi

- Cauliflower
- Broccoli
- Chinese cabbage
- Pak Choi

Many other vegetables can perfectly complement your rabbits' diet. However, keep in mind that leafy plants are the best food for rabbits and everything else should be fed secondarily. For example, tuberous vegetables have quite a lot of calories in comparison, so they should be used sparingly (e.g., carrots, even if some famous rabbits always munch on a carrot). Also, of course, fruit has many calories due to the high sugar content, although fruit is not unhealthy. Therefore, fruit is best used as a snack between meals or as a treat.

Examples of other healthy vegetables (as a supplementary food, please, not as a main food):

- Fennel (soothes the tummy)

- Bell pepper (without the green stalk)

- Tomato (without the green stalk)

- Carrot (gladly with carrot green)

- Spinach (not much because of the oxalic acid)

- Cucumber (especially in summer a great source of water)

Examples of fruit (not much please, more like a treat):

- Apple

- pear

- Strawberry (especially good: the green leaves)

- raspberry

- Watermelon (great in summer; also, the green or white parts)

- Peach (without pit)

- Grape (also the stems)

Typical Behaviour

The behaviors of rabbits are sometimes very different from the behaviors of other animals or humans. Therefore, many gestures and sounds are often misinterpreted. The following is a brief overview of common behaviors of a rabbit to avoid misinterpretation in the future and to interpret the behavior correctly.

Eating feces:

It is quite normal for rabbits to eat their own feces from time to time. This is the so-called appendix feces. As in humans, the rabbit's food passes from the mouth into the stomach and then into the small intestine. But the rabbit has another station: the appendix. This is where vitamins and nutrients are utilized. Appendicitis feces are often eaten by rabbits (and other species) - this is normal and healthy. You should only be concerned if a rabbit consumes a noticeable amount of feces. This may be a sign that it is not getting enough nutrients from its diet and needs to "get" them elsewhere. Or the rabbit may have an increased need due to an illness.

Riding up, mounting, jumping on:

A group of rabbits has a hierarchy - only one can be the boss and the following rabbits also form a hierarchy, at least while the hierarchy is still clear. In the wild, many rabbits live in fairly large groups, so there is also a hierarchy, but not too rigid a hierarchy, but in home enclosures, there are usually much smaller groups or pairs living together, so the animals can easily remember the hierarchy. Now, when one animal mounts another, it doesn't always have anything to do with reproduction or other needs - females also mount each other to find out who is the higher-ranking animal. If a rabbit climbs on the back or the rear end of another rabbit, this shows I am higher in rank than you. For humans this may sometimes be difficult to understand, but for rabbits (and also for many related animal species) this is completely normal. Humans should not interfere with this (unless it comes to biting), because the rabbits themselves must be allowed to clarify who is the boss with them.

Aggression against other rabbits:

Not all rabbits have a good relationship with each other, just as not all people get along. Sometimes it is a matter of luck (or rather: bad luck). If you adopt several rabbits together, which also lived together before, this risk is minimized of course, even if it can always come to a quarrel. Also, if the animals have lived together from an early age, there is less risk of aggression because the animals have known each other for a long time and are used to each other. Therefore, if one wants to carry out a socialization, it should be well observed. In general, however, rabbits are quite peaceful animals. In addition, it is also possible that aggression is due to a general indisposition, for example, because the animal is sick. We all know it: if we feel unwell and/or in pain, we are usually also more sensitive and often lose our nerves more quickly. It is the same with rabbits.

Sudden secretion, often accompanied by loss of appetite:

The animal may be sick and in pain. A competent veterinarian should be consulted if there is a sudden negative change in behavior. Many animals, such as the rabbit, try to hide pain and illness at first so as not to appear weak. This is due to their nature.

Beeping:

Rabbits do make sounds, but they do not use as many different sounds as other animals. For example, guinea pigs, which are also extremely popular pets, have a much greater variety of sounds with which they communicate with each other.

As a result, rabbits and guinea pigs have a hard time "talking" to each other. But now let's move on to the whimpering: whimpering is heard from young animals calling for their mama. Adult animals seldom whimper, but this sometimes occurs when they feel uncomfortable or frightened.

Hissing:

These sounds are usually very clear even to a human: the rabbit feels threatened or it is unhappy. It wants to be left alone and have its peace.

Growling:

Mating animals growl at each other when they are ready to mate. Humans are not usually growled at, as this would be unnatural behavior. Nevertheless, rabbits that must live in solitary confinement are observed to growl at their owner from time to time, since there is no other rabbit in the animal's solitary life and the rabbit must therefore consider the human as a caregiver.

Teeth grinding:

Teeth grinding can have two reasons, which could not be more different - on the one hand, the rabbit could be in pain. But on the other hand, rabbits sometimes grind their teeth when they feel comfortable and relaxed.

Standing still straight, "freezing":

The rabbit has sensed something, possibly danger, perhaps an unfamiliar sound or smell. The animal is alert and analyzes the situation. Usually, it runs away to avoid a possible danger first, but if there is no possibility of escape, it freezes and usually straightens its ears.

Stand on hind legs, make male:

When a rabbit does male, it is especially alert and wants to explore its surroundings "from above" to get a better view. However, rabbits also use this gesture to ask their owners for something: for example, a treat.

Tapping the ground with the hind legs:

Tapping with the hind legs is a well-known gesture for rabbits and is used in case of danger to alert other rabbits of an enemy or similar. Therefore, it is also common for rabbits to tap the ground when they feel lonely or frightened. It is thought that tapping may also serve to relieve stress, as the stress factor is high in the above situations and it has been observed that females willing to mate sometimes also tap, even though they are not frightened - so it probably also serves to relieve stress.

Digging, burrowing:

Digging and burrowing is a natural behavior for rabbits because in the wild they often dig long underground tunnels. Of course, this is not possible in domestic rabbits; nevertheless, domestic rabbits should also have a way to pursue their burrowing instincts. For this reason, it is recommended that rabbits be provided with at least one burrowing box.

Mutual grooming:

It is natural for rabbits to groom each other - this shows their affection and strengthens their bond with each other. It is often observed that rabbits groom each other's faces and around the ears; this is a proof of love in many species.

Socialization

A socialization can become necessary due to many events, for example when a group or a pair is put together at the very beginning of keeping and cannot be obtained from one source or when a rabbit unfortunately dies, and a new rabbit is to move in. Compared to some other species, most rabbit socializations usually go quite peacefully if you follow a few rules. Please keep the following in mind when socializing:

1. neutral ground

Please don't just put the new rabbit into the enclosure, because this usually overwhelms both the new rabbit and the old rabbit (or: the old rabbits) and often leads to arguments, because a too abrupt change takes place. The socialization should always take place on neutral ground, be it in a separate enclosure, on the living room floor covered with blankets or similar. This way not only the new rabbit has to face an unfamiliar situation, but also the old rabbits are on new ground and usually do not act as dominant as when an intruder suddenly stands in their own territory. Socialization in the territory can lead to fierce disputes in which the rabbits sometimes even fight each other to the death.

2. health

A socialization is always associated with stress, so it should only be "expected" healthy rabbits. Also, of course, it should be ensured that the new rabbit does not have any diseases that it could introduce. Therefore, it is advisable to have a fecal sample tested on all animals prior to socialization; and at best, the E. Cuniculi status should also be determined in the blood of all animals.

3. time and patience

How long a socialization takes, cannot be said in general. With some rabbits it goes very quickly, they get along well right away and can also clarify the ranking uncomplicatedly. With others, it takes longer, the solution drags on and perhaps some rabbits are also very shy. This is always a matter of character, and it depends on how the characters of the individual rabbits fit together. It is not uncommon for socialization to take a few days or even weeks; only then should they move back into "normal territory". Animals should not be separated at night, as this can delay the socialization process, for example if the animals have to "start all over again" afterwards.

4. enough space and hiding places

The rabbits should not be crammed together, but it is important that they can set their own pace and also get out of each other's way if necessary. For this reason, at least one house (or similar shelter) is also necessary per rabbit so that they can retreat. Ideally, these houses should have two entrances, because if another rabbit comes in, a scuffle is avoided, and the animal can use the other exit. While some recommend not using hiding places so that the animals are forced to fight with each other, I do not recommend this. Rabbits are flight animals and will panic if there is no hiding place nearby. A socialization is already stressful enough, so you should give the animals the time they need and allow them to withdraw from time to time.

5. food and water

In any case, the rabbits should be provided with plenty of food and water. The food is best distributed in several places so that this does not create additional potential for quarreling. The food serves as an occasional distraction, to "take a break" and it can also strengthen the bond when the animals eat together. After all, food makes you happy (not just people, but rabbits too). The better the rabbits know each other, the closer they are likely to sit together while eating, too.

6. persevere

It is not advisable to put the rabbits apart and back together more often, as this simply slows down the process. Also, constant back-and-forth is even more stressful for the animals. Therefore, if possible, the socialization should proceed from start to finish without interruptions and at the end all rabbits can move into the enclosure together (provided there are no bloody bites, wedging, and the like).

7. intervene only if there is biting / blood flowing or similar.

This point is quite difficult for many people, because one feels sorry for the rabbits - especially for the inferior rabbit. But one should intervene really only in the emergency if the animals bite each other hard or even blood flows. As long as the animals behave normally - i.e., run after each other, chase each other, mount each other - you should not intervene, as this only prolongs the process unnecessarily. The animals then start all over again when they are put back together, and this is even more tiring. It is perfectly natural for these animals to have a hierarchy, so we should not anthropomorphize them. The rabbits will probably stand in front of each other with their teeth chattering, they will raise their little heads, they will jump up to show each other that they are strong. They will probably mount each other, usually from behind, sometimes from the side or front. All of this is normal and necessary to figure out which rabbit should be on top or bottom of the pecking order. However, if the rabbits bite into each other, if there is blood or the like, the human should intervene.

8. moving into the "right" enclosure

After a lot of chasing, riding, etc., the hierarchy will eventually become clear. The inferior rabbit will signal to the new "boss" that it is submitting by lying flat and letting the dominant rabbit ride and/or groom it again. Over time, they will become closer and closer, such as sitting next to each other while they feed. When the rabbits get along well, they can move to their "real" enclosure - together. However, socialization on neutral ground should last at least 4-5 days, even if it seems to be already completed. It is recommended to clean the enclosure thoroughly beforehand and use fresh textiles or fresh litter. It is also a good idea to move the enclosures around so that everything is nice and fresh.

9. later attempts to change the ranking order

Even though the order of precedence is initially established, this does not mean that it can never change. There are rabbits that try to move up in rank, so there may be fighting, chasing, and climbing later on. Sometimes they succeed and the ranking is changed. However, this is rather rare and shifts usually occur again only when, for example, a rabbit dies.

© *Alex S. Goodlynx*

Common Diseases

All people and animals can get sick. Some get sick more often, others less often. Animals such as rabbits are not immune to disease, of course, and the severity ranges from "very mild" to "potentially fatal." However, how often and how severely a rabbit becomes ill depends in large part on how well the animal is kept and how it is fed.

As with us humans, disease prevention is key - a rabbit that is kept species-appropriate, has enough space and exercise, whose needs are met, and is fed a balanced and healthy diet, will most likely not get sick too often.

Of course, even with perfect husbandry, certain diseases can occur, for example, through heredity (often due to questionable breeding practices; genetics!) or sheer bad luck. However, the vast majority of animal diseases are caused by the animal owner - not intentionally, but usually due to simple ignorance of optimal husbandry conditions.

Among the most common mistakes in terms of husbandry and nutrition are, for example ...

... high-calorie industrial feed, too little fresh feed;

... too little exercise (e.g., due to lack of space);

... Stress (e.g., due to no harmony in the group, quarrels, humans handling the animal too roughly, etc.);

... Fears and loneliness (rabbits are social animals!);

... Dehydration (no fresh drinking water; not enough fresh food).

Not every little thing requires a visit to the vet. A visit to the vet is always stressful because the rabbit is taken out of its familiar environment and has to face a very stressful and exhausting situation that can sometimes last several hours, including the drive.

Nevertheless, I advise against self-treatment and self-medication for liability reasons. Especially with beginners, there can be misjudgments and mistreatments, because they do not have much experience with rabbits yet. I therefore point out that diseases must always be recognized and treated professionally by a competent veterinarian.

When choosing a veterinarian, make sure that he or she has experience with rabbits. This should be an absolute must. A reputable veterinarian will only treat a rabbit anyway if he or she feels confident to do so based on experience and can help the animal professionally.

Of course, the owner must be sensitized to the detection of diseases. If you know your animal, you will notice quite quickly if something is wrong and if the animal changes. Not every little change has to be a sign of a disease, but the following signs often indicate a disease - especially if they occur in a combination ...

... Loss of appetite, refusal to eat;

... Diarrhea;

... sudden aggressiveness and irritability (often a sign of pain);

... unnatural movements;

... Changes in the shape, color, and/or consistency of the feces;

... Loss of pleasure in movement;

... Changes in the eyes (watery, glazed or similar).

Although a disease is a case for the veterinarian, the owner should basically know about the different diseases. Therefore, we will now take a closer look at some rabbit diseases.

Unfortunately, there are specific rabbit diseases that are very serious and can kill hundreds of animals very quickly on rabbit farms, for example. However, these diseases can also affect pets. These are on the one hand myxomatosis (also called "rabbit plague") and on the other hand RHD (also called "China plague"). As with vaccinations with us humans there are also in this connection vaccination proponents and vaccination critics. Meanwhile, in some countries even quite rabid pro and contra "camps" have formed. A vaccination of course, as with humans, always carries certain risks, but in the end, it depends on whether the advantages or the disadvantages outweigh. In the case of the above-mentioned rabbit diseases, the advantages of vaccination outweigh the disadvantages in my opinion, also because rabbit diseases are diseases that almost always lead to death in the case of an infestation. In some vacation accommodations and similar accommodations for rabbits even only vaccinated rabbits are accepted.

However, it should be said that not all vaccines are approved in all countries and veterinary recommendations can vary from country to country and sometimes from region to region - so be sure to consult your veterinarian about vaccinations against myxomatosis and RHD and get competent advice. The intervals between vaccinations are also important to consider - a competent veterinarian will advise you on this in detail.

- Myxomatosis:

Myxomatosis can be transmitted through many different routes, so even with careful hygiene, it is not impossible for this infectious disease to break out, because the routes of infection are through people and other animals as well as through food and insects. Especially due to the transmission by insects it can hardly be controlled, and the pathogens can be transmitted by rabbit fleas, flies and mosquitoes. Myxomatosis is triggered by the poxvirus. By far not only rabbits kept outdoors are in danger, but also rabbits living indoors, especially because flies and mosquitoes find their way into houses during the summer months. In most cases, the disease ends fatally (even with treatment), so I advocate vaccination - if action is taken immediately, emergency vaccination may still save the rabbit's life, but the risk is still very high.

Symptoms include, for example, the formation of myxomas (nodules), conjunctivitis, mucus in the respiratory tract, and swelling of mucous membranes (e.g., eyes, genital area).

- RHD:

The abbreviation "RHD" stands for "Rabbit Hemorrhagic Disease" and it is a calicivirus that exclusively affects rabbits and hares. Like myxomatosis, RHD is also fatal in the vast majority of cases. Also the ways of infection are similar, because RHD is also not only transmitted from rabbit to rabbit, but unfortunately also by insects and food, therefore I advise also here to a vaccination, in order to protect the animals - even with the best hygiene and caution - reliably, because there is unfortunately still no effective medication against RHD; for this reason the preventive protection by a vaccination is the safest. RHD usually leads to the death of the diseased animal even more quickly than myxomatosis.

Symptoms differ from those of myxomatosis - for example, common symptoms of RHD disease include blood clotting disorders and leakage of blood from various body orifices, as well as bloody diarrhea, and also cramps, fever, and respiratory distress.

- RHD2:

As the name suggests, RHD2 (Rabbit Hemorrhagic Disease 2) is a variant of the previously explained viral infection RHD. This new variant was first identified in 2013 and has since spread from France around the world. Regrettably, this variant also leads to the death of the diseased rabbit in almost all cases.

RHD is a nasty and almost always fatal disease, but RHD2 unfortunately strikes even more brutally. RHD2 causes even more severe damage to the rabbit's organism and when a rabbit becomes infected, death occurs in many cases within a few hours. It has often been observed that no signs of disease could be detected with RHD2 because this variant of the virus takes the rabbit so quickly.

Another major difference from the original variant, RHD, is that there is no bleeding - previously we explained that in RHD disease, blood comes out of the orifices. In RHD2, sometimes, for example, fever and apathetic states occur, but these symptoms can also be caused by other diseases - therefore, RHD2 is usually not identified in time, also because sick rabbits die so quickly. Also, for these reasons vaccination is highly recommended.

We have now taken a closer look at the three current rabbit diseases that rabbits can be vaccinated against. Now let's look at some more common diseases.

- Diarrhea

Diarrheal disease can have a variety of causes. In rabbits, we speak of diarrhea not only when the feces are watery, but also when the shape and/or consistency of the feces has already changed significantly. Healthy feces are uniformly round. The consistency is firm and almost dry. Diarrhea also weakens the animal so that the rabbit is tired, does not seem as active as before, and/or consumes less food and water. Cloudy eyes and weight loss may also occur.

Diarrhea must be taken very seriously because the animal can quickly become dehydrated. Especially if the rabbit refuses to eat and if the diarrhea lasts longer than a day, urgent action should be taken (veterinarian). The most important point is to provide the rabbit with extra fluids - if it does not drink enough, it should be fed extra fluid-rich foods.

The most common causes of diarrhea are:

1. a change in food too quickly - any change in food should be done slowly. Don't offer your rabbit too much of a new food at first but increase portions slowly. This is especially true for fresh food that the rabbit has not yet experienced.

2. moldy or fermenting food - For this reason, food should always be checked before feeding to make sure it does not show signs of mold. Also, food debris should be removed from the enclosure daily.

3. worm infestations or other parasites - small worms can often be seen on feces with the naked eye, but feces should always be examined and analyzed by a veterinarian if a parasite infestation is suspected.

4. Poisonous Plants or Plastic Parts - If the rabbit comes in contact with poisonous plants in the home and gnaws on them, this can lead to symptoms of poisoning, often accompanied by diarrhea. The same is true for gnawing on plastic parts.

5. Stress - When the rabbit is exposed to stressful situations, the animal can be under tremendous psychological strain. A battered psyche can affect physical health and often manifests itself in digestive problems - usually diarrhea.

- Colds

Colds must be taken very seriously in rabbits. The small body is not as robust as, for example, that of humans, so that a cold can also very quickly lead to a dangerous pneumonia, which in the worst case is fatal. A cold must therefore be counteracted very quickly since the aggravation usually occurs much faster than in humans. The symptoms are the same as in all mammals: Colds are manifested by sneezing, a runny nose, watery eyes, rattling breath, and similar cold symptoms. To avoid colds, drafts should be avoided entirely. Also, the rabbit should not be exposed to excessive temperature fluctuations. Nevertheless, of course, care should always be taken to ensure that the room is well ventilated. Stress or lack of hygiene can also promote colds. The transmission of pathogens often takes place through humans, so you should take good care not to infect the rabbits when you yourself have a cold. Also, a weak immune system naturally favors - as with us humans - the outbreak of a disease. This is another reason a healthy, varied, vitamin-rich diet and enough exercise are so important.

- Fungal diseases

When a rabbit is infected with a fungus, in many cases you will find round hairless areas on the body. The skin is usually scaly or shows scabs. Fungal infections can also be accompanied only by hair loss - or scaly areas of skin can be found on the ears, eyes, or the like. Fungal infections can be caused by poor hygiene and lack of air circulation, but many animals also suffer from a fungal infection that has psychological causes. This may be due to too much stress, anxiety, loneliness or other negative feelings. Poor mental health also weakens the immune system, which can also lead to fungal infections.

For the layperson it is usually difficult to distinguish between a fungus, mites or similar. Therefore, a visit to the veterinarian is essential. Please also note that a fungus is contagious and can be transmitted to humans as well as to other pets. Therefore, hygiene is the first priority here as well.

- Tumors

Even the best cared for, and happiest rabbits can develop a tumor; even with the best health and excellent hygiene, it is possible for an animal to develop a tumor. Therefore, preventive care is extremely important. You should completely palpate your rabbits at regular intervals and look for hardened areas. If you notice an unusually hard spot under the skin or a small hard bump, you should visit the veterinarian and have this evaluated. A tumor may also need to be surgically removed; this will be decided by the veterinarian.

- Abscesses

Abscesses can easily be mistaken for tumors, especially if the abscess feels hard. However, unlike tumors, abscesses are collections of pus caused by bacteria. Similar to a tumor, an abscess can occur anywhere in the body. In most cases, abscesses are caused by external injuries such as bite wounds or cuts on sharp objects, pointed branches or the like. Bacteria can enter the body through the open wound and cause an infectious abscess. Also, if the animal scratches itself frequently and vigorously, an abscess can develop from these small skin lesions. This is another reason it is important to regularly palpate the rabbit and look for hard or enlarged areas on the body. Whether it is a tumor or an abscess (or a simple fatty growth (lipoma)) will be evaluated by the veterinarian. Not all abscesses need to be treated surgically; this is always a case-by-case decision. In either case, it is important that the pus be drained properly so that the abscess does not rupture and potentially cause blood poisoning.

- Heat stroke

In general, rabbits are uncomfortable at temperatures above 25°C and heat stroke may already be imminent if this high temperature persists for a long period of time - it can become very dangerous at temperatures above 28°C. Therefore, a normal room temperature (20°C or even cooler) is ideal for rabbits. Especially when keeping rabbits outdoors, this can be difficult to ensure depending on the region. In addition, rabbits should never be exposed to direct sunlight, at least not if they cannot move out of the sun at any time as soon as they get too warm. Please always make sure that the rabbits do not get too hot. If the rabbit suffers heat stroke, it will sometimes pass out or suffer from respiratory distress. This should not happen in the first place. Shallow side breathing or lethargy can also be signs of heat stroke. It is important to note that rabbits are barely able to cool their bodies down on their own, and because of this they are much more sensitive than us humans (or even than dogs, because dogs can pant). Rabbits can neither pant nor sweat; they are only able to let off a little heat through their ears, but this is usually not enough. In addition, fur retains additional body heat. Therefore, rabbits should not be exposed to high temperatures in the first place, and there must always be enough places for them to cool down - otherwise heatstroke can lead quite quickly to circulatory failure, which can cause the rabbit to faint and, in the worst case, even die.

- Misaligned teeth (malocclusion)

Malocclusions can be congenital or hereditary but can also be caused by an improper diet (not enough raw food, not enough fiber, not enough chewing, etc.). As teeth continue to grow, they must be worn down repeatedly by chewing, but this is sometimes more difficult with misaligned teeth. Affected animals often refuse food, sometimes they drool, sometimes infections occur in the oral cavity. Of course, these do not develop from one day to the next, but over many weeks or months. Therefore, it is recommended to check the teeth about once a week. During this check-up, the animals can also be directly palpated for possible tumors/abscesses and other abnormalities. If there are signs of dental problems, a competent veterinarian should be consulted as soon as possible.

- Parasites

Parasites are quite common in rabbits. A distinction must be made between endoparasites and ectoparasites.

The reproductive products of the endoparasites are excreted with the rabbit feces. Thus, they are located inside the rabbits. Ectoparasites, on the other hand, are found in or on the skin of the animal. They can also "burrow" into the skin. But how does a parasite infestation occur in the first place when rabbits are kept as pets isolated in the home and have no direct contact with other animals or the environment outside the home?

Either direct or indirect transmission of parasites occurs. Affected animals can transmit parasites to the other animals without any intermediary, for example, through physical contact or through the feces of the diseased rabbits. On the other hand, parasites can also be introduced into the group through objects or food. You can bring parasites from outside to inside on your shoes, they can be on your hands, they can be transmitted by flies and other insects. The risk can be reduced by good hygiene, but never completely eliminated.

In the event of a parasite infestation, it is important to examine and treat all animals in the group. Not all animals infested with parasites will also show outward symptoms. As with humans, the immune system of rabbits is quite variable, and some animals are more susceptible - especially animals that are more sensitive and easily stressed. It is very likely that the entire group is affected by the parasites, even if not all animals develop symptoms. However, if only the rabbits with external symptoms are treated, the parasites on/in the healthy rabbits will not be eliminated and could easily be re-transmitted.

Therefore, treatment of parasites should definitely be done by a knowledgeable veterinarian. This person will be able to clearly identify the type of parasite and initiate appropriate treatment methods. In the following, we will take a brief look at some of the most common parasites.

1. tapeworms belong to the endoparasites. The tapeworm lives in the digestive tract of rabbits and usually causes weight loss (sometimes extreme) and digestive problems such as constipation or

diarrhea. Tapeworms are usually transmitted to rabbits through intermediate hosts, such as mites or fleas.

2. fur mites belong to the ectoparasites. When infested, rabbits usually suffer from itching and sometimes dandruff. The itching occurs mainly in the head area and on the back.

3. hair follicle mites also belong to the ectoparasites. Due to the hair follicle mite infestation, the animals often lose hair or fur, and the skin usually turns dark; especially in the head and back area. Hair follicle mites are extremely small and therefore cannot be detected without a microscope.

4. coccidiosis (endoparasites) occurs most often in young animals - or also in old, immunocompromised animals. The animals

usually suffer from diarrhea and lose a lot of weight. The diarrhea causes the body to dry out quite quickly, which in the worst case can lead to the death of the animal. Since these are endoparasites, a fecal examination is mandatory. Thereupon, the expert veterinarian will treat the infestation with appropriate medication.

5. scabies mites, like all mites, belong to the ectoparasites. In the case of an infestation of scabies mites, the itching from which the animals suffer is extremely severe. The frequent and excessive scratching usually causes severe sores on the body. Bald patches in the fur are also common. Scabies mites occur in most cases in other animals, so these parasites are usually transmitted from other pets to the rabbits. As a preventative measure, it is recommended that each rabbit be weighed approximately once a week, teeth checked, and the entire body briefly palpated for any unusual areas.

© *Juli Reichel*

Frequently Asked Questions

Do I have to keep my rabbits indoors? Can't I also keep them outside?

Yes, you can. However, there are a few more points to consider. 1.

1) The minimum dimensions, which we have already discussed in the chapter "Enclosure", should be guaranteed in any case also in outdoor housing. Therefore, rabbits should not be kept in small rabbit hutches, which are often offered in the trade for outdoor keeping. The hutches available in the trade are almost all much too small. However, a rabbit hutch can of course be additionally integrated into the enclosure.

2. the enclosure must be secured from all sides - not only from the side, but also from above and

below. This is very, very important. From above, for example, birds of prey could spot the rabbits and snatch them. You can't look that fast! Also, from below the enclosure must be completely secured - because otherwise, for example, martens can burrow under the grid! (Example: aviary wire, washed concrete slabs - a predator must not have the possibility to bite through). It should also be noted that rabbits themselves naturally like to dig and that there is a possibility they could dig an underground passage to the outside. Therefore, many keepers resort to, for example, sidewalk slabs or the like.

3. rabbits that previously lived indoors and are to be relocated outdoors must not be shocked into cold temperatures. Therefore, it is advisable to accustom the rabbits to living outdoors during warmer months, so that they can gradually get used to the changing temperatures as it gets a little cooler day by day.

4. in case of wind and rain, the enclosure must be protected with tarpaulins or similar, unless the rabbits live permanently in a wind-protected place anyway, such as a converted gazebo. If you have an outdoor enclosure, there must be at least one shelter so that the rabbits can seek refuge from wind and weather there. For this purpose, for example, the previously mentioned rabbit hutches from the trade, but also children's playhouses or the like.

5. rabbits need a lot of space, of course, but the previously mentioned shelter should not be too large, so that it does not cool down too much. A shelter half a square meter is enough for two rabbits, so they can warm it up together.

6. in the cold seasons, the enclosure must be cleaned especially often to avoid mold.

7. in summer, the rabbits must be protected from the burning sun and there must be enough shady

places. However, the heat must not accumulate in the enclosure!

8. since the temperature outside cannot be controlled, the rabbits must be offered further cooling in summer (e.g., cooling packs, shallow water baths, etc.).

Keeping rabbits outdoors is much more complicated than keeping them indoors and must be well planned and monitored daily.

© *Hans*

Do I need to shower or bathe my rabbits?

No, this is not necessary. Your rabbits do their grooming all by themselves and groom themselves thoroughly. Bathing would only be unnecessary stress for the animals and there is also a risk of catching a cold. It is different, of course, if the rabbit is very dirty in a certain area, for example, if it has had severe diarrhea (vet!!) and the anus is very dirty and sticky or if the paws are very dirty. Then, however, you should not bathe the whole animal, but best only the affected area (s) with a natural, fragrance-free means. Sometimes baby shampoo without chemical additives is also suitable.

Should I also feed my rabbits seeds?

Seeds/seeds or dry food in general should not make up the bulk of the diet, but should only supplement it, if at all. The rabbits' natural diet remains greens (and hay), but some seeds can supplement the diet well. For example, sunflower seeds are little fatteners as they are very high in fat, but they are fantastic as a treat as they keep the skin nice and supple and prevent dehydration, for example. Small amounts of the following oilseeds are also suitable as treats or supplementary food (examples):

- Nettle seed
- fennel seeds
- anise seed
- linseed
- black cumin
- Sesame seeds

When are rabbits most active?

Rabbits are not bound to a specific time of day, however, it is often observed that these animals are quite active at the twilight hours (i.e., dawn and dusk). Therefore, they are counted among the crepuscular animals.

Why do my rabbits sleep so little?

It probably just seems that way to you. Rabbits don't sleep for a long period of time at a time (like we humans do) but alternate between the waking state and the sleeping state much more often.

In addition, rabbits don't always sleep with their eyes closed. Sometimes they are open or only half closed. Only when a rabbit feels completely safe and senses no danger whatsoever does it close its eyes completely. But this also depends on the day.

How many hours a day do they sleep in total?

Rabbits, as previously mentioned, do not sleep for many hours at a time. This is because, for example, as prey animals, they must always be on guard. Even though they are not exposed to danger in our homes, they are and remain flight animals that retain their instincts. Therefore, rabbits spread their short naps throughout the day and night, often totaling as many as thirty separate naps. Adding up all the short naps, most rabbits sleep between eight and twelve hours a day.

How old did the oldest rabbit in the world become?

The oldest rabbit probably lived to be 18 years old. There have been some very old record holders among rabbits over time; the most prominent are:

1. Do was a rabbit of the American breed "Jersey Wooly". He lived with his keeper in New Jersey, USA and died at the age of 17 (1996-2013).

2 Mick was an Agouti rabbit who lived in Illinois, USA. He turned sixteen in 2019 and subsequently received an entry in the Guinness Book of World Records.

3. Flopsy turned a handsome 18 years and 10 months old. He lived in Australia, however (unlike the two rabbits above) he was a wild rabbit that was captured in 1964 and then kept as a pet.

Can I keep my rabbits in a cage if they get daily exercise?

No, please don't. Unfortunately, commercial cages are far too small, and rabbits should always have the opportunity to follow their urge to move - and not only when humans allow it. Conventional cages can, of course, be integrated into the enclosure or serve as a toilet, but they should never be the rabbits' primary living space. In addition, as previously discussed, rabbits do not sleep continuously at night (as we humans do), but also need the opportunity to move around extensively at night.

Dear Readers ♥

For independent authors, product reviews are the foundation of a book's success. That is why we depend on your reviews.

This helps not only the authors, but of course also future readers and especially the animals!

Therefore, I should be grateful for a little review on this book. Thank you so much for your support! 😊

I wish you all the best, much joy with your rabbits and stay healthy!

© Vi Jakob

Legal Notice

Author: Alina Daria Djavidrad

Contact: Wahlerstraße 1, 40472 Düsseldorf, Germany

1st edition (2022)

© Celine Martin CJMM

Room for Notes

Printed in Great Britain
by Amazon

13014285R00081